ALI THE

A Potted P...
(in rhyme)

by

C. R. COOK

SAMUEL   FRENCH

LONDON

NEW YORK   TORONTO   SYDNEY   HOLLYWOOD

CHARACTERS

(in the order of their appearance)

THE NARRATOR
ALI THE BARBER
A "DONKEY"
AL BALONI, the Robber Chief
HASSAN, Ali's son
A CUSTOMER
MARY ANNA, the heroine, Ali's slave
MRS ALI
UNCLE CASSIM (curse 'im)
CHORUS OF ROBBERS AND DANCING GIRLS

SYNOPSIS OF SCENES

PRODUCTION NOTES

THIS "potted panto-parody" is played in curtains. It can be performed equally well by a mixed cast or an all-women cast. The Narrator can be of either sex, should read his lines, and act as Prompter. The Customer can be one of the Robbers, and the "Donkey" two of the Dancing Girls in donkey-costume, or be simply a child's toy on wheels.

Six or eight Robbers, and Dancing Girls, are sufficient. It is quite fun if the Robbers and Dancing Girls are in fact played by the same people, some of either sex. As Robbers they could have turbans and false beards, and cover their Dancing-girl costumes with cloaks and gum-boots, etc. Cassim may also re-appear in Scene 5 as a Dancing Girl, if he likes.

Costumes can be improvised from wide-sleeved blouses, boleros, and baggy pyjama trousers gathered at the ankles, with wide sashes round the waist. Turbans can be made from scarves or coloured towels. The Dancing Girls, of course, should have bare midriffs, and wear baggy trousers, of fine net or butter muslin, gathered at the ankles, over bathing trunks.

Al Baloni should be large and powerful, and Ali rather small. Mary Anna is young and sweet. Hassan is young, but rather a dolt.

Four or five rehearsals should be sufficient.

ALI THE BARBER

SCENE I

SCENE—*Outside the Robbers' Cave.*

THE NARRATOR *appears in front of the* CURTAIN. *He may, but need not, be in costume. He carries a gong and striker.*

NARRATOR.
Good evening, friends. We think it's time
That we put on a pantomime—
And so we'll put the matter right—
Regardless of expense—tonight!
We'll tell of love and greed and passion!
Poetic Dramas seem the fashion,
And so our little pantomime
Has throbbing rhythm, ruthless rhyme,
A Chorus too—in fact, the Lot!
What else has T. S. Eliot got?
So now, without any further ado,
I'm honoured and proud to present to you
A magical tale of the mystic East,
A dazzling vision of splendour, a feast
Of mirth and music—with silken swirls
Of a legion of luscious dancing girls! *
Of a fabulous Treasure Cave of gold,
And forty bandits, bad and bold,
And . . . Well, I think we can skip the rest—
If you didn't know, I expect you've guessed
It's "Ali The Barber Of Baghdad"!
And in Scene One, for business is bad,
Ali's out in the forest, gathering wood—
He doesn't do that when business is good.

* *If you can persuade a well-known gentleman to sit near the front and to stand up immediately on the cue "dancing girls", insert here an extra couplet:*
> "Sit down, Mr . . .—they're not on yet!
> You'll see them later, sir—Don't fret!"

By chance he has chosen the very place
Where, hidden in a bare cliff-face,
Is the entrance to the Robbers' Cave!
That's all!
(*He strikes the gong*)
          Pull up the curtain, Slave!

THE NARRATOR *goes. The* CURTAIN *rises. The stage is
bare, apart from a few scattered twigs on the floor, for Ali
to pick up. The cave entrance may be a gap in the curtains
back* C, *which is opened when necessary by invisible hands.
Or screens may be used, the "opening" being effected by
moving one of the flaps from behind.* ALI *enters* L, *with
a partly-filled sack, and a* DONKEY. ALI *picks up a few
twigs and puts them in his sack, then stops* C, *and introduces himself to the audience.*

ALI (*to the audience*)
Hullo, you people—let's be pally!
I'm just a poor barber—name of Ali.
I keep a barber's shop in town.
Haircutting, shaving—half a crown!
But modern fashions are very weird,
Every young Teddy-boy grows a beard!
So barbering in Baghdad is no joke—
In fact today I'm almost broke!
A bag of coal costs seven and six—
And so I'm out here gathering sticks,
While my boy Hassan looks after the shop.
So pardon me, now—I mustn't stop.

(ALI *goes on gathering. If the* DONKEY *is human, it may
perform a comic Dance now, if you like. After a while,*
ALI *straightens up, and stands listening, hand to ear*)

Hullo—what's this sound I hear?

(*There is complete silence*)

(*Louder*) Hullo—what's this sound I hear?

(*There is the sound, off* L, *of galloping horses*)

A band of horsemen drawing near!

(*He looks off* L)
How wild they look! How fast they ride!
They must be robbers—I'd better hide!

(ALI *and the* DONKEY *hide in the wings* R. BALONI'S *voice is heard off* L)

BALONI (*off*)
Whoa! Dismount, my men!

(*The sound of galloping ceases.*)

                  Wait here,
And I'll see if the coast is clear.

(AL BALONI, *the Robber Chief, enters* L, *and introduces himself to the audience*)

'Evening, all! I'm Al Baloni.
I've just arrived upon my pony.
I'm chief of forty robbers bold,
Who scour the countryside for gold.
(*Confidentially*)
This secret cave wot you can't see
Is where we 'ides our L.S.D.
Inside the cave, all unsuspected,
Is all the treasure we've collected!
There's bags of Ruby's, piles of Pearl's,
And diamonds too, from other girls,
Gold in chests, and fivers in sacks—
Today you call it "Income Tax"!

(SONG, BALONI. *Tune: "Solomon Levi"*)

Oh, my name is Al Baloni, I'm the leader of a band,
A band of forty brigands, who terrify the land.
We take your gold and valuables, we plunder all
     you've got—
We rob the rich, we rob the poor, we rob the
     blinking lot!

(*As* BALONI *sings the refrain, the* ROBBERS *march in,* L, *and join in the repeat refrain*)

Bold Al Baloni! Tra la la la la la—
Brave Al Boloni! Tra la la la la la la la la la la—
His name is Al Baloni, he's the leader of a band,
A band of forty brigands . . . (*etc.*)

(DANCE *optional. Each* ROBBER *carries a sack, clearly labelled* "Swag", "Loot", "Gold", *etc. At the end of the second refrain,* BALONI *shouts:*)

Robbers, fall in!

(*The* ROBBERS, *sacks on backs, line up* L *of the cave door.* BALONI *stands* R *of the door*)

           Thieves—attention!
While I the magic words will mention.
Close your eyes so you can't see!

(*The* ROBBERS *close their eyes*)

Hands over ears!

(*The* ROBBERS *put their hands over their ears*)

(*He shouts to the cave door*)
           "Open, Sez Me!"

(*The cave door opens*)

Robbers, right turn! Through the secret arch,
Deposit your luggage inside. Quick *march!*

(*As the* ROBBERS *march into the cave,* BALONI *ticks them off with a large pencil on part of a roll of paper, which he unwinds as he counts aloud* "One, two, three," *etc. up to thirty-nine. He can miss out a lot of the numbers to save time, but the* ROBBERS *must keep running round the back and coming on again, as necessary, until* "thirty-nine" *is reached. Should one too many arrive, he can say* "thirty-nine and a half". *He then rolls up the roll, counts* "forty" *and enters himself. The cave door closes behind him.* ALI *and the* DONKEY *emerge from their hiding-place*)

ALI.
     Well, well! This is a big surprise.
     Why! I can hardly believe my eyes.

They're wicked men without a doubt!
And I have found the thieves' hide-out,
Their treasury hid by secret doors,
The robbers' Quarter-Master's Stores!
Now, when they've gone, I'll slip inside
And see what wealth these cliff-walls hide.
I'll claim, perhaps, just *one* of the sacks
As rebate on my Income Tax.
'Tis sure *I* have more need than they!
They're coming back! I'll hide away!

(ALI *and the* DONKEY *hide off* R. *The cave door opens, and* BALONI *comes out first, followed by the* ROBBERS, *without their sacks. You can do the ticking-off business, as before, if you like, but it isn't really necessary. The cave door closes behind them*)

(SONG *and* DANCE, ROBBERS *and* BALONI. *Tune: "Tramp, Tramp, Tramp! The Boys Are Marching"*)

ROBBERS (*singing*)
We're Baloni's robber band, we're the terrors of the
    land,
And we hope you understand the tale we tell!
You must do as you are told, you must hand us all
    your gold,
And your watch and chain and valuables as well!

Tramp, tramp, tramp! Baloni's marching!
Look out, Baghdad! Here we come!
If you haven't got a groat, we will simply cut
    your throat!
For we love the sight of blood!—but keep it mum!

In the middle of the night, it would give you all a
    fright
If you chanced to meet Baloni's robber band.
In the woods, keep out of sight! We don't care,
    'cause *we're all right!*
For we're wealthy men, and life is simply grand!

Tramp, tramp, tramp! *etc.*

BALONI (*shouting*)
To horse, my men!

(*The* ROBBERS *file out* L. BALONI *consults a little note-book*)

Now who have I missed?
Ah! . . .'s * the next on the list!

(BALONI *exits* L. *Noise of galloping horses, which fades away.* ALI *and the* DONKEY *enter* R)

ALI.
They've gone away, so all is well.
And now *I'll* try the magic spell.
"*Open, Sez Me!*"

(*The cave door opens*)

It works! Hurray!
This is a game that *two* can play!

(ALI *goes into the cave, returning almost immediately with a bag of gold in each hand. The door closes behind him*)

This will settle those unpaid bills!
Oh boy! There's gold in them thar hills!

CURTAIN

SCENE II

SCENE—*Ali's barber shop.*

THE NARRATOR *appears in front of the* CURTAIN.

NARRATOR.
So while friend Ali homeward hurries,
With two sacks of gold to end his worries,
We'll take a look at his barber's shop,
Where Hassan, his son, with razor and strop,
And scissors and things, whatever they use,

* *Insert the name of a local person well-known for his wealth.*

Is striving to fill his father's shoes—
As brave as Horatius, if not braver,
He holds the bridge!—a bright young shaver!
For Hassan is young, just seventeen,
And madly in love—and he hasn't a bean!
And . . . Well, curtain up! and you shall see—
The barber's shop!
(*He strikes his gong*)
               "*Open—Sez Me!*"

The Narrator *goes. The* Curtain *rises. A* Customer
is sitting c, *with his back to the audience.* Hassan *is busy
lathering the Customer's face, with a large whitewash-
brush.*

Hassan (*to the audience*)
I'm Hassan, Ali the Barber's son,
And this is where the work is done.
Perm and set your beard? It's easy—
I'm the Persian "Teasie-Weesie"!
Have you tried the "Penny Bun"?
Watch it grow—it's really fun!
The "Miranda Line"? Now, that's a wow!
Why go to . . .'s? * Really, now!

(Hassan *has finished lathering, and now begins to shave
the Customer with a large wooden razor, or toy dagger.
His next lines are addressed to the* Customer, *who grunts
after every sentence. If you can add some local gossip, in
rhyming couplets, do so by all means*)

Lovely morning, sir! I hear
The farmers had a lousy year!
You read what Eden said to Ike?
They say the Cabinet's going on strike.
They want more pay—it's money for jam!

(*The* Customer *yelps*)

Sorry, sir! I really am!
Things look black in the Middle East.
Well, Malta's always there, at least!

               * *Insert the name of a local hair-dresser.*

Did you back that horse I tipped?

(*The* CUSTOMER *yelps again*)

Sorry, sir—the razor slipped!
(*He goes on shaving*)

(MARY ANNA *enters* R, *with a broom. She sweeps a little, then turns to the audience*)

MARY ANNA (*to the audience*)
I haven't come here for a shave.
I'm Mary Anna—Ali's slave.
I come from a Problem Family—
The youngest daughter of sixty-three.
I led a very sheltered life
Till father married his seventeenth wife—
And then there wasn't room for me,
So he sold me to Ali for one and three.
I cook the meals and lay the table,
And sleep with the donkey in the stable.
I work all day, from breakfast till supper—
In my spare time I'm the sweeper-upper.
(*She goes on sweeping*)

(HASSAN *removes the cloth from around the* CUSTOMER, *who stands up, still with his back towards the audience*)

HASSAN.
There you are, sir! You look fine.
That will be just two and nine.
CUSTOMER (*paying Hassan; savagely*)
You expect a tip now, I suppose.
You've had it already! The tip of my nose!

(*The* CUSTOMER *turns round, revealing a very uneven beard, only half a moustache, various bleeding wounds, and the tip of his nose missing. He stamps out* L, *dabbing his wounds.* HASSAN *sadly sits astride the now vacant chair* C)

HASSAN.
Oh dear, the outlook's very bleak—
The *only* customer this week!

My chance of TV fame is gone—
There's not enough clients to practise on!
No tip at all—not even a tanner!
This is dreadful, Mary Anna!
Just two and ninepence in the till,
And four poor hungry mouths to fill—
And I'm saving up to marry you!
My sweetest, what are we to do?

MARY ANNA.
But your father! However much you save
He'd *never* let you marry a *slave*!
But darling Hassan, don't despair!
Don't worry! Put away your care.

(SONG, MARY ANNA: *Any modern "cheer-up, keep smiling"
kind of song.*)

(ALI *enters* L, *greatly excited, carrying his two sacks of
gold*)

ALI.
Hassan! Hassan!

HASSAN.
                What is it, Pop?

ALI.
Lock the door, son! Shut the shop!

(HASSAN *locks the door* L)

Cheer up, Hassan, don't look so glum—
Hurry up and fetch your Mum.

(HASSAN *exits* R)

Oh, Mary Anna, I'm so excited!
Won't Mrs Ali be delighted!
Draw the blinds, girl—carefully—

(MARY ANNA *draws imaginary blinds*)

We mustn't let the neighbours see.
(*He opens the sacks of gold*)
Look, we're rich! Two sacks of gold!
Oh, what a tale can I unfold!

No more haircuts, singes, shaves—
I'll buy another dozen slaves—
Yes, my girl, that's what I'll do—
And they can all work under you!

(MARY ANNA *weeps tears of joy*)

Hush, this is no time for grief.
MARY ANNA.
Promotion! Oh, I'm Slave-in-*Chief*!

(MRS ALI *and* HASSAN *enter* R)

ALI.
Mother! Hassan! Look! It's gold!
(*He holds up the sacks*)
Farewell, hunger! Goodbye, cold!
Handsome Hassan, loving Wife—
Bags of gold! We're rich for life!
MRS ALI (*wonderingly*)
Am I dreaming? In a trance?
(*Realization*)
Ali! You've won the Treble Chance!
ALI.
Well, wife . . . that's not *exactly* true—
But for the present, perhaps will do.
MRS ALI.
The things I'll buy! A TV set,
A washing-machine and fridge I'll get!
A saucepan-set in best enamel . . .
HASSAN.
And I can buy a racing camel!
Oooh, won't I have a lot of fun!
MRS ALI.
Exactly *how* much have you won?
ALI (*lamely*)
Er—just a couple of bags or so.
How much? I don't exactly know!
We'd better count it, I suppose.
MRS ALI.
Count it, Ali? Goodness knows
How long 'twould take to count *that* treasure!

We'll have to use a two-pint measure.
(*To Hassan*)
Go to your Uncle Cassim's, son,
And see if he can lend us one.

HASSAN.
Uncle Cassim? That cunning old crook!
I think you're making a big mistook!

MRS ALI.
I know he's a rogue—but he lives next door,
And he won't know what we want it for.

HASSAN.
A two-pint measure. Okay, Mum!

(HASSAN *exits* L)

ALI.
And now, my dearest Wifie, come!
We'll celebrate in a fitting manner.

(ALI *takes a gold coin from one of the bags and gives it to Mary Anna*)

Buy a crate of Champagne, fair Mary Anna!

MARY ANNA (*excited*)
Champagne, master? What a thrill!
(*She recovers her dignity, and bows gracefully*)
Thy Slave-in-Chief performs thy will!

MARY ANNA *makes a stately exit* L. ALI *and* MRS ALI
watch her go, smiling, as—

the CURTAIN *falls*

SCENE III

SCENE—*Ali's living-room.*

THE NARRATOR *appears in front of the* CURTAIN.

NARRATOR.
Now everything seems fine and swell.
But that's not the end—as you know very well!

For with Scene Three, there "comes the dawn"!
It's after breakfast, the following morn.
The gold is measured, and safely stowed,
And Ali's paid the debts he owed,
They've ordered a fridge and a TV set,
And other small things they wanted to get,
And Mary Anna's got promotion! . . .
When—ah! *Who comes?* You have no notion?
Listen! In Ali's living-room,
We hear the steps of approaching doom!
The Fly in the Ointment!—Yes, *that's him!*
Their no-good Uncle—the greedy Cassim!
Who wants . . . Ah, well! Get on with the play!
Ready, behind there?
(*He strikes the gong*)

            Take it away!

THE NARRATOR *goes. The* CURTAIN *rises on an empty stage.* UNCLE CASSIM, *who chews gum, pokes his head round the door* L.

CASSIM (*calling*)
Ali! Hassan! Anyone here?
(*He comes in to* C)
Hassan! Ali! This is queer.
(*To the audience*)
I'm Ali's brother, Cassim the Cunning.
I never work for two days running.
I live on my wits—and I've plenty of those!
I sponge on my friends and I swindle my foes.
Why *work*, when a little investigation
May inspire a vivid imagination
To work out means of easy money?
For instance, now—here's something funny!
Yesterday, Hassan, Ali's son,
Borrowed a measure—a two-pint one.
To measure what? A sack of wheat?
Or rice? Or something else to eat?
In that case, where did they get the dough?
(*Wickedly*)
Ha! Brother Cassim means to know!

And so . . . Well, what would *you* do, chum?
(*Craftily*)
A little piece of well-chewed gum
Adhering to the measure's bottom—
(*Triumphantly*)
And clever Cassim's *got* 'em—rot 'em!
(*He shouts*)
Ali! Hassan! Anyone in?

(HASSAN *enters* R)

HASSAN.
Goodness me, what is this din?
(*Without enthusiasm*)
Oh, Uncle Cassim. What a pleasure!
CASSIM.
Have you finished with my measure?
HASSAN.
I think so. I'll just ask my Mum.

(HASSAN *exits* R)

CASSIM.
Ha! At last! The hour has come!

(MRS ALI *and* HASSAN *enter* R. MRS ALI *carries a measure*)

MRS ALI.
Morning, Cassim. How d'you do?
This is an early hour for you.
Lovely weather, is it not?
Here's your measure. Thanks a lot.
(*She hands him the measure*)
CASSIM (*aside*)
Now to find out what Ali bought!
Let's see what fish my bait has caught!
(*He puts his hand in the measure and pulls out a gold coin*)
What's this? A guinea! What a prize!
Can I really believe my eyes?
(*To Mrs Ali*)
Madam, has Ali *so* much treasure
He has to count it with a measure?

(MRS ALI *stands speechless with amazement*)

Come, speak up, madam. Are you dumb?

HASSAN (*quite happily*)

You made a mistake—I *told* you, Mum!

MRS ALI (*to Cassim*)

Well, yes, you see, he has—in a way—
But he only got it yesterday.
He set off at nearly half past six,
And went to the woods to gather sticks—
'Cos yesterday was very cold—
And came back last night with two sacks of gold.

HASSAN.

We think he's won the Football Pools.

CASSIM.

Then you're a pair of stupid fools.
Football Pools! Don't be so wet!
They haven't been invented yet!
Now where's your husband, my brother Ali?
I *must* see him, particu-*lalli*.

MRS ALI.

He's gone to the Market with Mary Anna
To buy twelve slaves and a grand pianner.
He's got some idea that we ought to dine
With music, dancing-girls and wine.

CASSIM.

Well, if he turns up before half-past . . .

(ALI *and* MARY ANNA *enter* L. ALI *has a posh new
turban and a new sash*)

Ah, Ali! Here you are at last!
What's this I hear of sacks of gold?

ALI (*placidly*)

I don't know yet. What have you been told?

CASSIM.

Don't palm me off with silly chat
Of football pools and things like that.
I'm not a fool! I want the truth!

ALI.

All right, Cass. Don't be so uncouth.
It's a kind of Income Tax rebate——

CASSIM (*angrily*)
Now look here, Al—just get this straight . . .

(ALI *silences him with a gesture*)

ALI.
Cassim, there's no need to bawl.
Now gather round, and I'll tell you all.

(*They gather round Ali*)

(SONG, ALI.* *Tune: "John Brown's Body"*)

ALI (*singing*)
Walking in the forest, I was gathering some sticks,
And then I heard them coming, and I was in a fix!
Baloni and his robbers, in wild and thrilling ride—
So I thought I'd better hide!

HASSAN, MRS ALI *and* CASSIM (*singing the refrain*)
Goodness, gracious! Al Baloni!
Al Baloni on his pony!
Goodness, gracious! Al Baloni!
Whatever did you do?

ALI.
They rode up to a cliff-face—I hid behind a tree—
And then the bold Baloni shouted "Open—sez me!"
I saw the cliff-face open, large and deep and wide—
Then they disappeared inside!

HASSAN, MRS ALI *and* CASSIM.
Goodness, gracious! Al Baloni! . . . *etc.*

ALI.
Now when the thieves departed, I thought I'd go
    and see,
I stood before the cliff-face, and said "Open—sez
    me!"
There were sacks of gold and precious stones of
    every shape and size
Before my very eyes!

* *If Ali cannot sing, he may either recite the words in time with the
music, or simply recite the verses with no music at all, in which case, no
chorus is sung either.*

HASSAN, MRS ALI *and* CASSIM.
  Goodness, gracious, what a treasure!
  What a treasure! What a pleasure!
  Goodness, gracious! What a treasure!
    And then what did you do?

CASSIM (*excited*)
  Al Baloni's treasure cave, you say!
  How much gold did you take away?
ALI.
  Not counting the bonus I gave to my staff,
  Just five thousand and thirty-two pints and a half!
  But don't worry, Cassim, there's so much there
  They'll never miss *our* little share.
  We'll split it with you—won't we, Wife?
  And we'll *all* be rich for the rest of our life!
  So sit down, brother, and relax—
  En-*joy* your rebate of Income Tax!
CASSIM (*bitterly*)
  Rich! When you think of what's left behind?
  Oh, it's all right for *you*! But I'm not that kind!
  I'll go myself, to see, come what may,
  What *twenty* donkeys can carry away!
ALI.
  But, Cassim! We've got plenty enough!
  Besides, it's dangerous! Those brigands are tough!
MRS ALI.
  Ali is right. No need to be rash.
  We certainly don't need any more cash.
MARY ANNA (*prophetically*)
  Your greed will bring you nothing but sorrow!
CASSIM (*slowly*)
  I know what I'm doing. I'll go tomorrow!

CURTAIN

SCENE IV

SCENE—*Inside the Robbers' Cave.*

THE NARRATOR *appears in front of the* CURTAIN.

Narrator.
   And now Scene Four: The very next day—
   To the heart of the forest we wend our way;
   For Cassim, whatever else he's lacking,
   Is certainly quite a dab at tracking!
   Though greedy and grasping, he isn't a dunce—
   He made a very good Wolf Cub—once!
   With twenty donkeys strung behind,
   This human bloodhound means to find
   The robbers' gold! With vicious zest,
   He sticks his head in a hornet's nest!
   We're waiting now *inside* the Cave.
   He'll soon arrive—the greedy knave!
   I think I can hear his donkeys bray.

   (*Loud brays are heard off*)

   We're in the Cave!
   (*He strikes his gong*)
                              On with the play!

The Narrator *goes. The* Curtain *rises. Round the walls
   of the cave are various crates and sacks, plainly labelled
   "Diamonds", "Silver", "Gold", "Rubies", etc. There
   is also an empty sack in some convenient place. The magic
   door is* L.

Cassim (*off* L)
   These footprints lead to the cliff-face—
   I think that this must be the place!
   Now what were those secret words? Let's see—
   Er—yes! I remember!
   (*He shouts*)
                      "*Open, Sez Me!*"

   (*The magic door opens.* Cassim *comes in slowly, looking
   round. The door closes behind him, by itself*)

   Well, well! At last! The end of the trail—
   And I feared it was only a fairy tale!
   (*He reads*)
   "Diamonds", "Silver", "Gold", and "Rubies"—
   These robbers must be simple boobies!

This Al Baloni's an ignorant chap,
And Brother Ali! What a sap!
(*He opens various sacks, gloats over their contents, and
then begins to pile a few up in a small heap* c)
There's even more here than I thought!
Those twenty donkeys that I brought—
I'd better load them up in here.
I'll *have* to come again, that's clear.
I bet old Ali will be sorry!
I wish I'd brought a three-ton lorry!
(*He goes to the door*)
Now the magic words I'll shout,
To open the door and let me out.
"*Open, Sez You!*"

(*Nothing happens*)

                    Not loud enough?
(*Louder*)
"*Open, Sez You!*"

(*Still nothing happens*)

                    Say, this is tough!
Perhaps I haven't got it right.
"*Open, Oh Yeah!*" Still shut tight!
"*Open . . .*" Oh blow! I can't recall
Those wretched secret words at all!
(*He bangs wildly on the door, then stops*)
Now let me think—I mustn't panic.
I wish I were a skilled mechanic.
I should have brought some T.N.T.
Whatever will become of me?

(*The sound of galloping horses approaching*)

Ooooh! The robbers are coming back!
I'd better get into a sack.

(CASSIM *gets into an empty sack, feet first, at the back of
the stage. He pulls the mouth of the sack over his head. The
galloping sound ceases, and loud donkey brays are heard*)

Baloni (*off* l; *shouting*)
  Who left these twenty donkeys here?
  Dirty work afoot, I fear!
  Draw your swords and we shall see.
  Ready, men? "*Open, Sez Me!*"

(*The cave door opens.* Baloni *and the* Robbers *enter* l,
swords in hand. They stare at the pile of sacks c)

  Someone's pulled our loot about!
  Scatter, men, and search him out!

(*The* Robbers *march round, prodding the sacks with their
swords, until they find* Cassim, *who pokes his head out of
the sack when prodded*)

A Robber.
  Here he is!
Robbers (*together*)
              The lousy thief!
  Haul him up before the Chief!

(*The* Robbers *drag* Cassim c, *throw him on the pile of
sacks, then form a semi-circle around* Cassim *and*
Baloni)

Baloni.
  Who are you that dare invade
  Our secret precincts, and to raid
  The lawful proceeds of our trade,
  By hard and honest labour made?
Robbers (*together*)
  You villain! Robber! Bandit! Thief!
  Let us slit his gizzard, Chief!
Cassim.
  Spare me! I am not a crook—
  I only came to have a look!
Baloni.
  Lying knave! Have you no shame?
  Tell me, villain, what's your name?
Robbers.
  Villain! Robber! Thief and bandit!
  Kill him now! We cannot stand it!

Cassim.
    My name is Cassim. I'm not bad!
    I'm just a poor but honest lad!
Robbers.
    Cassim? Curse 'im! Curse 'im! Cassim!
    Knife 'im! Shoot 'im! Drown 'im! Gas 'im!
Baloni.
    Don't get excited, comrades—wait!
    While I ponder on his fate.
Robbers.
    Lying villain! Soon you'll rue it—
    You know you didn't oughter do it!

(Song, Robbers. Tune: "What Shall We Do With a
    Drunken Sailor?" As they sing, they dance around Cassim
    waving their swords, while Cassim weeps and Baloni
    ponders)

Robbers (singing menacingly)
    What shall we do with a Nosey Parker? (repeated,
        3 times)
        Early in the morning.

(Refrain)
    Hooray!—we've caught a traitor (3 times)
        Early in the morning.

(Extra verses)
    String him up on the nearest oak-tree!
    Cut his throat and slit his gizzard!
    Chop his liver in little pieces!
    Carve him up with a bacon-slicer!

Baloni.
    Enough of this frivolity!

(The singing and dancing stops)

Prisoner, come here to me.

(Cassim crawls to Baloni)

Tell me now, you snivelling knave—
How you learnt to get into this cave.

CASSIM.
　I'm innocent! So please don't scold me!
　My brother, Ali the Barber, told me!
BALONI.
　Ali the Barber? Indeed—forsooth!
　Where does he live? Now tell the truth.
CASSIM (*surprised*)
　Where does he live? Well, bless my soul!
　In the *only* house with a barber's pole!
BALONI.
　Right! Well, that's about all, I guess.
　Take him outside, men—we don't want a mess.
　Give him the works! Procedure "A"—
　"Operation *Mincemeat*"—straight away!
ROBBERS.
　Exterminate him! Give him hell!
　More sausages for . . . * to sell!

(*The* ROBBERS *exit* L, *dragging* CASSIM, *who wails.
When they are all out, except* BALONI *himself, there is a
scream, a gurgle and a cheer off*)

BALONI (*to the audience*)
　Number *one* gone! Now for the other—
　Number Two—his barber brother!
　There's one more Scene—don't go away!
　They'll soon learn "Crime Doesn't Pay"!

CURTAIN

SCENE V

SCENE—*Ali's living-room.*

THE NARRATOR *appears in front of the* CURTAIN. *He
carries his script.*

NARRATOR.
　So greedy Cassim has got his deserts!
　He's sausage-meat!—and I hope it hurts!

　　* *Insert the name of a local butcher.*

Sorry this play is rather gory!
But that can't be helped—it's part of the story.
Still . . . Well, shall I tell? I think I will!
(*In a stage whisper*)
Cassim's not *really* dead! He's not even ill!
(*Sepulchrally*)
A pool of scarlet lies under the trees!
(*Brightly*)
But it's only Red Ink!
(*He shouts over his shoulder*)
                    Hey! Charlie,* please!

(CASSIM *pokes his head through the* CURTAINS)

CASSIM.
    Want me, Fred? *
NARRATOR (*to the audience*)
                There you are, you see!
(*To Cassim*)
    It's all right now, Charlie.*
CASSIM.
                 Okay. Cheerie!

(CASSIM's *head disappears*)

NARRATOR (*referring to his script*)
    Now where's the place? I think that *this* is!
    But what of Ali? And his missus?
    And Hassan too? And Mary Anna?
    For Al Baloni's a crafty planner!
    By ruthless means he now will strive
    To murder *everyone* alive
    Who knows the secret of his cave.
    The situation's very grave!
    The Final Scene:—Three days have passed—
    And Al Baloni strikes at last!
    We're back in Ali's house once more,
    Where, unaware of what's in store,
    And quite oblivious of his doom,
    Ali sits with his wife in the living-room,

---

* *Replace by the actual Christian names of the actors concerned.*

Fondly imagining he's in clover!
Curtain up!
(*He strikes his gong*)
          Let's get this over!

THE NARRATOR *goes. The* CURTAIN *rises. There are four chairs side by side along the back wall. On two of them sit* MRS ALI, *who is knitting, and* ALI, *who is reading a sporting paper.*

MRS ALI.
Ali, now that you've retired,
Some useful hobby is required.
ALI.
Yes, dear. It *had* occurred to me.
Er—I thought of standing as local M.P.
MRS ALI.
Excellent, Ali! A good idea, that!
ALI.
I'll see this bloke . . . * and have a short chat.
I'll have to get rid of that barber's pole.
Where's Hassan?
MRS ALI.   He's just gone out for a stroll.
I wish that boy would settle down!
All day he tore around the town
Upon his racing drom-e-*dary*,
It was most extraordin-*ary*!
Women screamed and children yelled—
I think that camel's jet-propelled!
If only he'd find a quiet young wife
Who'd teach him to lead a sensible life!

(HASSAN *dashes madly in* L)

HASSAN (*excitedly*)
I bet you can't guess where *I've* been!
MRS ALI (*to Ali*)
You see, my dear, *that's* what I mean.
HASSAN.
Mother! Father! Have you heard?

* *Insert the name of your local M.P., or some well-known local big-wig.*

MRS ALI

    Hassan, don't be so absurd.

HASSAN.

    Uncle Cassim's *disappeared*!

ALI (*rising up*)

    This is exactly what I feared!

HASSAN.

    Someone saw the ugly toad
    Going along the forest road
    With twenty donkeys in a row—
    And that was *three whole days* ago!

ALI.

    I was *afraid* that he would ride out
    To find the wicked robbers' hide-out!
    (*Solemnly*)
    A stubborn man will never bend
    To take the counsel of a friend.
    I gave him more than he could spend . . .

HASSAN (*eagerly*)

    D'you think he came to a sticky end?

MRS ALI.

    Oh Hassan, darling—*do* shut up!
    When you talk like that I feel all *cut up*!

(MARY ANNA *enters* R)

ALI.

    Well, Slave-in-Chief, what is it, dear?

MARY ANNA.

    Good master, there's a stranger here
    Who asks that he may speak with thee—
    He craves thy hospitality.

ALI.

    Fair Mary Anna—go ahead!
    Show him in.

(MARY ANNA *exits* R)

          Ne'er be it said
    That Ali e'er refused his aid
    To under-dog or under-paid.

(MARY ANNA *shows in* BALONI R, *then exits.* BALONI
now wears an easily-removable false beard. MRS ALI
rises)

Pleased to meet you, sir, I'm sure.
Er—haven't we met some place before?
Could it have been at . . . * College?

BALONI.

No, indeed. Not to my knowledge.
A boon I beg of you, kind sir,
To a benighted travel-*ler*.
Although I'm not well-known round here,
My name's Abdul Bul-Bul Ameer—
An honest merchant, sir, I swear,
Who travels round to sell his ware.
I couldn't get in at the *Railway* † *Hotel*,
And the *Bull and Bush* † is full as well.
I wonder, sir, perhaps you might
Just put me up for this one night?

ALI.

A commercial traveller—oh, I see.
(*To Mrs Ali*)
He should prove excellent company!
(*To Baloni*)
Why certainly, sir—there's room to spare.
Do you travel in ladies' underwear?

BALONI (*indignantly*)

I certainly *don't*!
(*The penny drops*)
                         Oh yes, of course!
I travel in—er—tomato sauce.
I've got some with me. Would you mind
If I left it in your yard behind?

ALI.

A pleasure, I'm sure. The gate's unbarred,
And there's plenty of room in our backyard.
Is there very much of it, Abdul Bul-Bul?

BALONI (*meaningly*)

Exactly thirty-nine barrels full!

* *Insert the name of a local college. For W.I. casts, use* "Denman
College"   † *Replace by the names of local hotels.*

MRS ALI.

> If you'll excuse me, I'll be looking
> To see how well the supper's cooking.
> (*Confidentially*)
> I keep an eye on what they do—
> Too many slaves *will* spoil the stew!
>
> (MRS ALI *exits* L)

ALI.

> Come, Hassan. We will help to stack
> All Abdul's barrels round the back.
>
> (ALI *and* HASSAN *exit* L)

BALONI.

> The simple fools! How easily caught!
> It's turned out easier than I thought.
> They little know that when I shout
> My band of robbers will jump out—
> And Ali and his family
> Will very shortly—cease to be!
>
> (BALONI, *chuckling, exits* L. MARY ANNA *enters* R, *and watches him go*)

MARY ANNA (*to the audience*)

> A most suspicious-looking stranger!
> I've a feeling we're in danger—
> Though how or why I'm not quite sure.
> Let me think a little more.
> There's something queer about those barrels.
> I heard one humming Christmas carols.
> I'm certain that another swore
> When I rolled it on the floor.
> 'Tis *very* strange tomato sauce!
> Unless, perhaps . . . Why, yes! Of course!
> Those barrels must have *men* inside!
> Now why should thirty-nine people hide?
> Unless, perhaps—each man's a Bandit!
> Ah! Now I begin to understand it!
> Our guest, then, must be Al Baloni—
> I *thought* his whiskers rather phoney!
> Some vile crime has the villain planned!
> Well, *now* we know just where we stand!

(MARY ANNA *exits* R.

ALI, BALONI, MRS ALI *and* HASSAN *enter* L. MRS
ALI *is wearing a large string of pearls, necessary only for
the rhyme*)

MRS ALI.
Supper won't be very long.
Do sit down. We'll have a song.

(*They sit on the four chairs.* BALONI *is between* ALI *and*
MRS ALI)

BALONI (*to Mrs Ali*)
Madam, what exquisite pearls!
ALI (*clapping his hands twice, and shouting*)
Bring on the Dancing Girls!

(*The luscious* DANCING GIRLS *dance on* R. *They perform
an Oriental Wobble Dance. At the end of their perform-
ance, they stand, half of them on either side of the stage,
swaying to the music, which continues.*

MARY ANNA *dances on* R, *with a dinner-knife in each
hand. She does a Solo Dagger-Dance. At the end of it, she
turns on Baloni, and forces him, at knife-point, to* C. ALI,
MRS ALI *and* HASSAN *rise in amazement*)

MRS ALI.
These slaves! It really is too bad!
Mary Anna, are you mad?
ALI.
This is but a sorry jest!
No way to treat an honoured guest!
MARY ANNA.
It's *Al Baloni* in disguise—
Right before your very eyes!
(*She pulls off Baloni's false beard*)
Seize him, girls, and hold him tight!
Justice will be done tonight!

(*Half a dozen* DANCING GIRLS *run up and grip Baloni's
arms tightly.* BALONI *makes no attempt to resist. He
merely laughs*)

BALONI.

>Clever! But not *quite* clever enough!
>(*He shouts*)
>Forward, my men, and do your stuff!

>(*There are muffled thuds, off* L)

>(*Louder*)
>Forward, my men, and do your stuff!

MARY ANNA.

>Clever! But not *quite* clever enough!
>Alas! However much you shout,
>Your band of Robbers *can't* get out!
>(*She goes to the front of the stage, and talks confidentially
>   to the audience*)
>Shall I tell you what I did?
>Around the edge of every lid
>I put a smear of Limpet Glue—
>(*She holds up a small tube of glue*)
>A one-ounce tube costs five and two.
>A thousand uses in the house,
>For handy man or handy spouse,
>Seals a joint or mends a tear,
>Obtainable almost everywhere!
>(*She throws a few free samples to the audience*)
>So don't forget, whate'er you do,
>*Always* ask for "*Limpet* Glue"!

>(ALI, MRS ALI *and* HASSAN *come forward*)

ALI.

>Mary Anna! You've saved our lives
>With a tube of glue and two dinner-knives!
>Caught Al Baloni and all his horde!
>Fair heroine—name your own reward!

MARY ANNA.

>Good master, my wish is a simple one—
>Permission to marry Hassan, your son.

ALI.

>Take him, my dear—he's a decent boy—
>And with our thanks, we wish you joy!

>(HASSAN *and* MARY ANNA *embrace*)

HASSAN.

  I *knew* the Old Man would turn up trumps!
  I'll buy a camel with *two* humps!

ALI (*clapping his hands twice*)

  Bring me my telephonic set!
  (*One of the* DANCING GIRLS *hurries out, and comes back with a telephone, which she hands to Ali. Never mind the wires*)
  There's a number I want to get.
  (*He puts the receiver to his ear. Into the telephone*)
  This is Ali the Barber. I want the Police . . .
  No, no! I haven't *got* a niece!
  The *Police*, I said . . . I've told you twice!
  P, O, Po—L, I, C, E, Lice . . .
  Is that the Police? . . . Send round a fleet
  Of Black Marias . . . Yes, toot sweet!
  We've caught Al Baloni and all his crew . . .
  No! *Baloni* . . . That's right, and the same to you!
  And listen! I know where he keeps his swag . . .
  No, three or four lorries—it won't go in a bag!
  There's jewels and things in gleaming mounds—
  And gold and silver . . . Yes, *millions* of pounds! . . .
  It's all in a cave . . . Yes, *I'll* open the door . . .
  You think so? . . . Oh well, I don't know what for!
  She'll want me tomorrow? . . . Right-ho, then!
    Where? . . .
  Buckingham Palace? . . . Okay, I'll be there.
  Be seeing you later, Fabian. Cheer-ho!
  (*He replaces the receiver. Wonderingly*)
  Blimey! *Sir* Ali! Well, what d'you know!

(THE NARRATOR *enters*)

NARRATOR (*to the audience*)

  Well, folk, all wrongs have been put right!

ENTIRE CAST (*together*)

  And now we wish you all "Good night!"

(SONG: THE ENTIRE COMPANY: *Any "Wedding-bells-soon" type of song*)

CURTAIN

FURNITURE AND PROPERTY LIST

SCENE I

On stage—Twigs

Off stage—Gong and beater (NARRATOR)
        Script (NARRATOR)
        Partly filled sack (ALI)
        Sacks labelled "Swag", "Loot", "Gold", etc. (ROB-
        BERS)
        Toilet roll, large pencil (AL BALONI)
        2 bags of gold (ALI)

Personal—AL BALONI: notebook

SCENE II

On stage—Chair and cloth for Customer

Off stage—Large whitewash-brush (HASSAN)
        Large wooden razor (HASSAN)
        2 bags of gold (ALI)

SCENE III

Off stage—Measure. *In it:* gold coin (MRS ALI)

SCENE IV

On stage—Crates and sacks labelled "Diamonds", "Silver",
        "Gold", "Rubies", etc.
        Empty sack

SCENE V

On stage—4 chairs
Off stage—Script (NARRATOR)
        Knitting (MRS ALI)
        Sporting paper (ALI)
        String of pearls (MRS ALI)
        2 dinner-knives (MARY ANNA)
        Tube of glue (MARY ANNA)
        Telephone (DANCING GIRL)

THE MUSIC

PERMISSION to perform the pantomime does not include permission to use copyright arrangements of music.

The following traditional airs fit the lyrics given in the text. They are all published by Messrs Francis, Day & Hunter Ltd.

John Brown's Body
Tramp, Tramp, Tramp, The
   Boys Are Marching
What Shall We Do With a
   Drunken Sailor?
Solomon Levi

MADE AND PRINTED IN GREAT BRITAIN BY
BUTLER & TANNER LTD, FROME AND LONDON
MADE IN ENGLAND